DISASTER ALERT!

Fukushima Nuclear Disaster

Rona Arato

Crabtree Publishing Company
www.crabtreebooks.com

DISASTER ALERT!

presented by:

Crabtree Publishing Company

www.crabtreebooks.com

Author: Rona Arato

Editors: Kathy Middleton, Wendy Scavuzzo

Indexer: Wendy Scavuzzo

Design: Tammy McGarr

Photo research: Crystal Sikkens

Production coordinator and prepress technician: Tammy McGarr

Print coordinator: Margaret Amy Salter

Cover: International Atomic Energy Agency (IAEA) experts and Tokyo Electric Power Co. (TEPCO) staff take part in the United Nations nuclear fact-finding mission inspection tour at Unit 3 of the Fukushima Dai-ichi nuclear complex.

Title page: A journalist checks radiation levels at the Fukushima Dai-ichi nuclear power plant almost a year after the nuclear disaster.

Contents: A boat sits on top of a building in Otsuchi, Iwate Prefecture, Japan, 10 days after the devastating Tohoku earthquake and tsunami.

Illustrations:
Jim Chernishenko: page 7
Shutterstock: page 6
Thinkstock: page 8
Wikimedia Commons: page 10

Photographs:
Associated Press: cover, pages 3, 9, 11, 13, 14, 15 (bottom), 17, 18, 20, 21 (top), 23, 24, 28
© KIM KYUNG-HOON/Reuters/Corbis: page 13 (top)
Keystone Press: ©ZUMAPRESS.com: pages 1, 7, 16, 19, 25, 30, 31;
    © FAME Pictures: page 15 (top)
Shutterstock: pages 26, 29
Wikimedia Commons: U.S. Marine Corps photo by Lance Cpl. Ethan Johnson: pages 4–5; U.S. Navy photo by Mass Communication Specialist 1st Class Jerry Foltz: page 21 (bottom); Leary, Pete: page 22; Tiia Monto: page 27

Library and Archives Canada Cataloguing in Publication

Arato, Rona, author
    Fukushima nuclear disaster / Rona Rarto.

(Disaster Alert!)
Includes index.
Issued in print and electronic formats.
ISBN 978-0-7787-1192-6 (bound).--ISBN 978-0-7787-1194-0 (pbk.).--
ISBN 978-1-4271-8941-7 (pdf).--ISBN 978-1-4271-8939-4 (html)

    1. Fukushima Nuclear Disaster, Japan, 2011--Juvenile literature.
2. Nuclear power plants--Accidents--Japan--Fukushima-ken--Juvenile literature. I. Title. II. Series: Disaster alert!

Tk1365.J3A73 2014   j363.17'990952117   C2013-907583-6
                                                       C2013-907584-4

Library of Congress Cataloging-in-Publication Data

CIP available at Library of Congress

Crabtree Publishing Company

www.crabtreebooks.com   1-800-387-7650   Printed in Canada/012014/BF20131120

Published in Canada
Crabtree Publishing
616 Welland Ave.
St. Catharines, ON
L2M 5V6

Published in the United States
Crabtree Publishing
PMB 59051
350 Fifth Avenue, 59th Floor
New York, New York 10118

Published in the United Kingdom
Crabtree Publishing
Maritime House
Basin Road North, Hove
BN41 1WR

Published in Australia
Crabtree Publishing
3 Charles Street
Coburg North
VIC, 3058

Table of Contents

From Natural Disaster to Nuclear Crisis

On March 11, 2011, a major earthquake shook the northeastern region of Tohoku, on the island of Honshu, in Japan. Striking at 2:46 p.m., the shaking from the earthquake lasted for five terrifying minutes. Survivors emerging from the rubble of crumbled buildings were dazed by the amount of damage the earthquake had caused. However, this was only the first stage of a three-part catastrophe.

An earthquake

The Richter scale is a system that measures the strength of earthquakes on a scale up to 10.0. The Tohoku earthquake, also known as the Great East Japan Earthquake, measured an incredible 9.0. It was the fifth-strongest ever recorded and was felt for hundreds of miles around. The entire island of Honshu—the main part of Japan—was actually shifted eight feet (2.4 m) closer to North America by the force of the deadly earthquake.

A tsunami

The epicenter, or the place where the earthquake started, was under the Pacific Ocean 80 miles (129 km) off the east coast of Japan. Sometimes an underwater earthquake can trigger a dangerous tsunami, or giant wave of water. The Tohoku earthquake created a wave up to 124 feet (37.88 m) high—about as tall as a 13-story building! Almost an hour after the earthquake struck, an area of about 217 square miles (561 sq km) was quickly covered by rushing water. Entire towns were washed out to sea.

A nuclear accident

Located directly in the path of the tsunami was the Fukushima Daiichi nuclear power plant. Despite safety systems at the plant that automatically shut down nuclear reactors during earthquakes, flooding from the tsunami disabled the power supplies and cooling systems of the nuclear reactors in the plant. Without the ability to cool down, the reactors experienced a meltdown—a catastrophic situation that released radioactive materials into the air and water.

Tohoku Earthquake

Earthquakes are a regular occurrence in Japan. Made up of thousands of islands, Japan is located in an area of the world known as the Ring of Fire. The Ring's outline follows along underwater trenches **and volcanic fields that surround the Pacific Ocean.** About 90% of the world's earthquakes happen in this region.

Pressure underwater

Earth's surface is made up of about 20 huge, and many small, **tectonic plates** that fit together like pieces of a giant puzzle. The place where two plates meet is called a fault line. The area where Japan's Tohoku earthquake developed is located where the North American and the Pacific tectonic plates meet. These two plates move toward each other very slowly, about 3.25 inches (8.3 cm) per year. The Pacific plate slides under the North American plate, dragging the lip of the North American plate slowly down with it. Stress, or pressure, builds up along the fault line. In 2011, the lip of the North American plate snapped back up releasing pressure built up over centuries. The stress, released as a wave of energy, moved through the ground creating an earthquake.

Tohoku earthquake facts

- Tohoku was a megathrust earthquake.
- Fifth-strongest earthquake since 1900
- Four foreshocks ranging from 6.0 to 7.2
- Three of the thousands of aftershocks measured over 7.0
- Shaking felt as far as 1,242 miles (2,000 km) away
- It made the planet spin a bit faster, shortening the length of Earth's days by 1.8 microseconds.
- Shifted Earth's axis about 6.5 inches (17 cm)
- Japan's second-strongest earthquake was in Kanto, in 1923, measuring 8.3.

Diagram of a Megathrust Earthquake

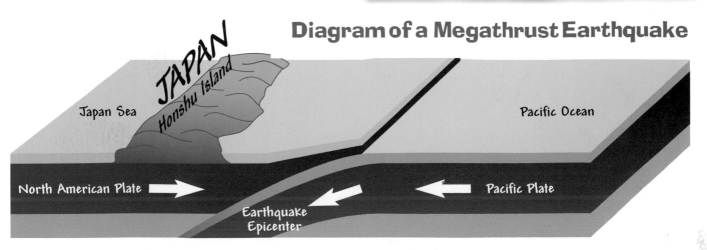

Japan Sea — JAPAN Honshu Island — Pacific Ocean

North American Plate — Pacific Plate

Earthquake Epicenter

Scientists are not able to accurately predict where and when an earthquake will strike. Japan does, however, have an early warning system for earthquakes. A warning to millions of people was sent by television, Internet, and text message to cellphones when **seismic waves** first occurred. In Tokyo, it gave people about one minute to move to a safe location before the violent shaking could be felt. The alert also gave time for high-speed trains to stop, gas lines to be shut off, and factories to shut down. Japan's strict building codes prevented massive damage to buildings from the earthquake.

Map of the Ring of Fire

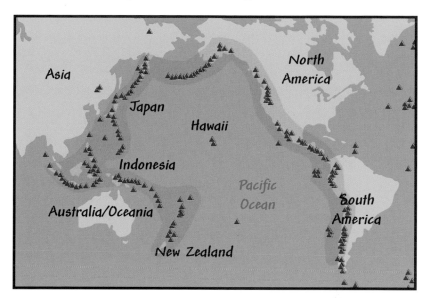

A hotbed of earthquake activity and volcanic eruptions, other major events in the Ring of Fire in recent years include the 7.1 Christchurch earthquake in New Zealand in 2010, and the 7.1 Santiago earthquake in Chile in 2012.

A search and rescue team carries an injured survivor to safety after the earthquake.

Tsunami Disaster

Not all underwater earthquakes trigger tsunamis. A tsunami occurs when an earthquake under the ocean is so strong that it suddenly shifts a massive amount of water. If the earthquake occurs in shallow water, as it did in 2011, the height of the waves intensifies.

What is a tsunami?

Tsunami is a Japanese word meaning "harbor wave." Tsunamis are triggered by an underwater earthquake or volcanic eruption. When an earthquake is strong enough to move the ocean floor, this violent movement shifts a massive amount of water that then rushes ashore as a giant wave. A tsunami is not one wave; it is a series of waves. The first wave is not always the most destructive. Tsunami waves can be up to 60 miles (97 km) long and arrive an hour apart. A tsunami wave can also cross an entire ocean without losing its energy. Issuing a tsunami alert takes longer than for earthquakes because important facts about the earthquake must be determined first. Quick, but inaccurate, warnings will lead people to not follow future warnings.

The force of the tsunami

The earthquake happened at a point where the ocean floor is only 15.2 miles (24.4 km) below the water's surface. The shallowness of the water, combined with the strength of the earthquake, caused a giant tsunami. Less than an hour after the earthquake, a massive wall of foaming white water smashed into Japan. The water raced inland sweeping away buildings, highways, bridges, and other structures. Boats were pushed into the cities, and cars and trucks crashed against buildings. Power lines came down. Many people had already fled to higher ground after the earthquake, but some had not. People fled to rooftops, while entire houses were pushed past them by water black with debris. Most who died in the Tohoku disaster were victims of drowning.

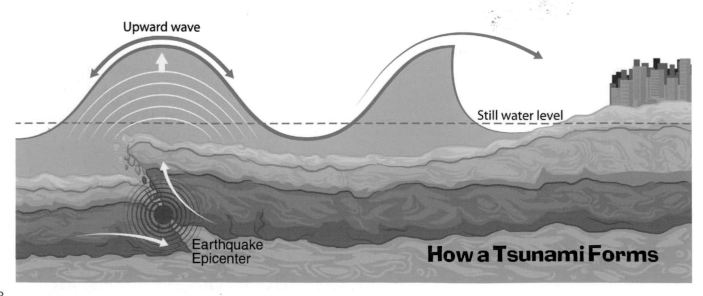

Upward wave

Still water level

Earthquake Epicenter

How a Tsunami Forms

(above) *A giant tsunami wave overwhelms homes in the city of Natori.*

In Oarai, a ship is caught in the swirling waters of a whirlpool created by the tsunami.

Facts about 2011 tsunami
- A tsunami warning was issued eight to 15 minutes before it hit the coast.
- Waves up to 124 feet (37.8 m) high
- Water came inland up to 6 miles (10 km).
- About 217 square miles (561 sq km) of land was flooded.
- Waves reached Alaska, Hawaii, and Chile—11,000 miles (17,000 km) away.
- The force broke ice slabs off the Sulzberger Ice Shelf in Antarctica.

Fukushima Nuclear Plant

Before the earthquake, Japan's 50 nuclear reactors had been generating 30% of the country's electricity. There are five nuclear power plants in the area of the Tohoku earthquake. At the time, 11 reactors were actively operating. The reactors were strong enough to withstand the earthquake, and all of the reactors in all plants in the area shut down automatically the way they should when an earthquake is registered.

What is a nuclear reactor?

A nuclear reactor is a piece of equipment designed to produce energy from **radioactive elements**. Uranium is the most common radioactive element, but plutonium and thorium are also used. Reactors are used for many purposes including scientific research, generating electrical power, and producing nuclear fuels and materials for medical procedures.

How does it make energy?

A boiling water nuclear reactor is like a giant electric steam kettle. It has a heating unit that heats water to produce steam. The uranium is contained in small ceramic, or clay, pellets inside long metal rods stored inside the reactor. These rods are kept in water to keep them cool so they do not overheat. If the rods get too hot, they can melt and release dangerous radiation.

A Boiling Water Nuclear Reactor

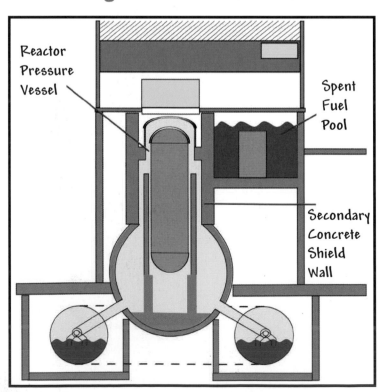

Reactor Pressure Vessel

Spent Fuel Pool

Secondary Concrete Shield Wall

Energy is produced by splitting the atoms, or tiny particles, of the radioactive material into smaller atoms. This is done inside the reactor by hitting an atom with a **neutron**. When the atom splits, it produces more atoms and neutrons which, in turn, hit other atoms and split them. This process, called fission, will continue as long as atoms are present. When an atom splits, it releases energy in the form of heat. It heats the water surrounding the rods and creates steam. The steam is used to turn turbines so generators can produce electricity.

Fukushima Daiichi facts

The Fukushima Daiichi power plant was first put into operation in 1970 in the town of Futaba. Operated by the Tokyo Electric Power Company, also known as TEPCO, the plant generated electricity for an area that included the country's capital, Tokyo. Fukushima Daiichi sits on a high, steep bank on the edge of the sea and houses six boiling water reactors fueled by uranium. At the time of the earthquake in March of 2011, only reactors 1, 2, and 3 were in operation. Reactors 4, 5, and 6 had already been shut down for maintenance.

Power plant vs nuclear bomb

Every time an atom splits, it releases energy. When many atoms split at once, it causes an explosion, which is what happens inside a nuclear bomb. But, in nuclear power plants, the number of atoms splitting is controlled because the rods absorb some of the neutrons, limiting the energy released. Nuclear power plants are not supposed to explode. To prevent leaks of neutrons, the reactor is surrounded by a concrete and steel building with walls that are 3 to 6 feet (1 to 1.83 m) thick!

This photo shows the buildings that house reactors 1 to 4 at the Fukushima Daiichi nuclear plant. Reactors 5 and 6, located to the right of this picture, as well as number 4 had been shut down for maintenance before the earthquake.

Nuclear Disaster

So what went wrong? Power at the Fukushima Daiichi plant failed after the earthquake, but emergency backup generators quickly took over. When the tsunami flooded the plant, the backup generators failed. Without power, operators could not control the cooling and water circulation functions of the reactors. The possibility that the reactors would overheat and experience a meltdown was high.

What is a meltdown?

The rods containing the radioactive material inside a reactor give off heat even when the reactor has been shut down. If the cooling system also shuts down and the water level drops, the fuel rods become exposed to the air. This causes the outer casings on the rods to crack and release fuel. If the fuel then heats up enough, it sinks to the bottom of the reactor and can burn through it, causing what is called a meltdown. A meltdown releases dangerous radioactive gas into the surrounding area, which can cause serious illness in people and wildlife, as well as poison the soil, water, and air.

The chain of events

When the tsunami knocked out Fukushima Daiichi's backup generators, operators turned to emergency battery power. Within eight hours, the battery power ran out, and again the system that cooled the rods in the reactors and the spent fuel pools, where used up pellets are stored, could not operate. Cooling water levels sank. The rods gradually became exposed to the air and continued to overheat. Over the next several days, three explosions occurred from a buildup of hydrogen gas inside the reactor buildings. Trucks and helicoptors attempted to cool the reactors with seawater. Despite these efforts, reactors 1, 2, and 3 each experienced a meltdown.

Timeline of Events at Fukushima Daiichi

2:46 pm (Japan Time)
- 9.0 earthquake strikes off the coast of Japan
- Active nuclear reactors automatically shut down
- Plant loses electricity, and backup generators take over

3:36 pm
- 42.5-foot (13 m) tsunami wave hits Fukushima Daiichi plant
- Plant is flooded and generators stop working
- Battery power takes over

9:00 pm
- Evacuation of people living within 1.9 miles (3 km) of the plant is ordered

3:36 pm
- Battery power is used up
- Hydrogen explosion destroys top of building housing reactor 1
- Spent fuel pool of reactor 4 is exposed to the air

9:40 pm
- Evacuation area expanded to 12.5 miles (20 km)

- Seawater is injected into reactor 3.

- Second hydrogen explosion destroys roof of building housing reactor 3
- Spent fuel pool of reactor 3 is exposed
- Seawater is injected into reactor 2
- 11 workers are injured

March 11, 2011   **March 12**   **March 13**   **March 14**

Smoke rises from the building housing reactor 3 as helicoptors drop large amounts of seawater to help cool down overheating fuel.

While these dramatic events were unfolding, ten percent of homes in Japan were without electricity or were experiencing **rolling blackouts**. More than 400,000 people were living in temporary shelters. The Japanese people, still reeling from the death and destruction of the earthquake and tsunami, were now facing a nuclear catastrophe and the possibility of poisoning from radiation.

On March 15, Emperor Akihito, the head of Japan's royal family, addressed the country on television. The emperor usually speaks only in times of extreme crisis. He offered words of encouragement saying, "I hope that those affected by the earthquake will not give up hope and strive to survive, while taking care of their health."

- Two more explosions damage buildings 2 & 4
- Reports of boiling water in spent fuel pool in reactor 4
- Cooling systems back in operation in reactors 5 and 6
- People living within 18.5 miles (30 km) advised to stay inside

- Helicoptors begin dumping tons of seawater on overheating reactors. This continues for weeks. Eventually, fresh water is available again for cooling.

- Reports of boiling water in spent fuel pool in reactor 3

March 15　　March 16　　March 17

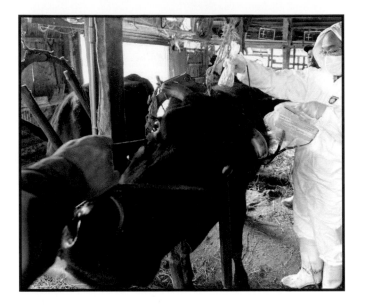

Dangerous levels

By March 18, the severity of the accident was raised by the International Atomic Energy Agency (IAEA) from level four to five on the International Nuclear Event scale. Level five is the same as Pennsylvania's Three Mile Island accident, in 1979. By April 12, it had been raised to an alarming level seven—equal to the world's worst nuclear accident, Chernobyl, in the former Soviet Union, in 1986. The world community watched with concern and offered assistance to Japan.

While workers were trying to contain the damaged reactors, scientists were continuously performing tests on air, water, and soil samples. Evacuation areas were expanded, and warnings issued to the public about drinking water, food sources, air, and soil when tests indicated there were unsafe amounts of radioactive contamination.

(Top) Livestock had to be left behind during the evacuation. Many animals on farms starved with no one to feed them.
(Bottom) Radiation levels and salt from ocean water made some soil impossible to farm. Some farmers have now switched to indoor farms using hydroponic methods.

- Shipments of cattle from Fukushima area banned

- Most people from Fukushima plant area allowed to return home

- Soil in affected areas not safe to farm. Rice banned after radioactive contamination detected

- Government announces leaking reactors have been contained
- It was determined that meltdowns had occurred in reactors 1, 2, and 3.

July 19 - August 25   September 30   November 15-16   December 16

Cold shutdown

By the end of the third week of the catastrophe, the immediate crisis had passed at Fukushima Daiichi. But it was mid December before the government officially declared the three reactors were in **cold shutdown** condition. For these damaged reactors, a cold shutdown meant that the temperature was below the boiling point of 212 degrees Fahrenheit (100 degrees Celcius) and radioactive materials being released into the air were not dangerous. The next step began which was to develop a plan to safely remove the fuel. In October of 2013, the first part of the plan was put into action and work began on moving fuel rods from the spent fuel pool in reactor 4 to safer storage in a pool on the ground at the plant. The plan calls for all fuel to be removed from the plant within ten years of the accident.

(Above) Temporary shelters were set up for people evacuated from the area.
(Below) With no fresh water available, seawater was used to cool the damaged reactors. The problem with seawater is that salt from the water can harden around the fuel rods making them harder to cool down.

Nuclear Cleanup

It took many weeks of work by hundreds of engineers, workers, firefighters, and military personnel to bring the reactors under control. Many had lost their own homes and, in some cases, their families. They risked their lives to prevent an even larger catastrophe.

Danger to workers

In the first few days of the accident, a core group of workers, who came to be nicknamed the "Fukushima 50," remained at the plant after the tsunami hit to work on the reactors, facing great danger from the escaping radiation. They were quickly joined by large numbers of firefighters and military personnel. Conditions were extremely hazardous, and they worked around the clock. While dozens of people were injured and three workers at the plant died during the reactor crisis—two during the tsunami and one of a heart attack—no workers died from exposure to radiation during the emergency. Long term, however, their exposure may affect their health in years to come. TEPCO came under criticism in the months after the disaster for the lack of safety equipment available to workers, such as dosimeters which measure workers' exposure to radiation, and inadequate training for subcontractors, or workers who were not employees of TEPCO.

Two years after the accident, reporters were allowed in to view the progress on the cleanup of the crippled Fukushima plant. Wearing protective gear, they viewed storage facilities being built to hold spent fuel rods.

At least 1.5 inches (4 cm) of topsoil must be scraped off contaminated land for disposal. Scraping all of the farmland surrounding Fukushima would fill 20 sports stadiums. Where to store at least 3.3 million tons (3 million metric tons) of soil is a difficult problem for the island nation.

The task of cleaning up the **contamination**, which is still ongoing, has proven to be enormously difficult. At the nuclear plant, dangerous materials, including fuel from the damaged reactors, water from the cooling systems, contaminated filters, equipment, and other debris, have to be collected and either stored safely or treated. Tons of contaminated soil have been scraped from the site of the plant and the surrounding evacuated areas. Perhaps the biggest challenge is finding a safe place to store

the many tons of contaminated material. As for reactors 1, 2, 3, and 4, the damaged structures surrounding them must be reinforced in the short term for safety, but all four will be decommissioned, or put out of operation. The fate of reactors 5 and 6 has not yet been decided by the Japanese government.

Helping Survivors

The search for survivors began immediately after the disaster. Japan's Prime Minister Naoto Kan sent 50,000 troops, 190 military planes, and 25 ships to help in the rescue and recovery efforts. Countries around the world joined the search.

Search for survivors

The Japanese government responded immediately to help victims, and aid poured in from around the world. Three Japanese groups—the Association for Aid and Relief Japan (AAR), Japan Emergency NGO (JEN), and Peace Winds Japan—received financial and technical aid from the International Rescue Committee. One of the main areas of concern was to rebuild the affected area's coastal fishing industry, which had been devastated by the disaster. Hundreds of thousands of people lost their homes, and the government committed billions to rebuild the areas the tsunami destroyed.

A tragic toll

According to an October 2013 report from the National Police Agency of Japan, 15,883 people were killed in the earthquake and tsunami disasters. Another 2,652 were missing and 6,149 injured. About 475,000 people had to be evacuated from devastated areas as well as from safety zones around the damaged nuclear plants. Approximately 126,600 buildings were destroyed and another one million were damaged. The earthquake and tsunami resulted in more than $300 billion in damage and economic loss for the people of Japan.

Hundreds of thousands of people were relocated from the affected area. Two years after the event, about 313,000 were still living in temporary housing or rented apartments.

Devastation in Sendai

The one million residents of Sendai had only eight minutes warning before the tsunami hit. An economic center of the northeastern region of Japan, Sendai is located 80 miles (129 km) from the epicenter of the earthquake. The city lay directly in the path of the tsunami that followed. The airport's security camera recorded the destruction by the raging water. The giant 33-foot (10 m) wave traveled inland up to 6 miles (10 km) smashing buildings on its way in and carrying the rubble on its way back out to sea. Police discovered hundreds of bodies on the beaches immediately afterward. The deaths would grow to thousands. Geological evidence shows that the Sendai area was devastated by a similar tsunami in the year 869—more than 1100 years ago.

A father and son survey the damage in Sendai.

Recovery in Japan

The challenges facing the Japanese people are enormous. Hundreds of thousands of people lost their homes. It will cost the government billions to rebuild the Tohoku region where the tsunami hit. There are also concerns about the nuclear cleanup. Is it effective? Will it repair the problems caused by the tsunami?

Two years later

All but two of Japan's 50 nuclear power plants are still not in operation, and the government has not yet decided whether to reopen them. Where many of the houses, businesses, and even some towns once stood, the ground is now completely bare. Although much of the estimated 250 million tons (254 metric tons) of debris has been cleared away and disposed of, many areas in Japan have still not been cleaned up. Disposing of the debris is a huge problem because there are not many places to put it.

Because Japan experiences so many earthquakes, most of the buildings in the country are built to strict codes, or regulations, to make them earthquake-resistant. It was the tsunami that had a far more devastating effect than the earthquake.

Japanese soldiers look for survivors in the rubble in Natori.

The triple disaster affected the whole country. Roads and transportation networks were destroyed or under mountains of debris. Industries could no longer produce goods that were sold locally and around the world. The economy of Japan and the economies of countries that trade with Japan all suffered.

A few months later, Japan's production and sale of goods was nearly back to normal, the country's economy was recovering, and its people were trying to rebuild their lives. Much of the farmland, however, was also contaminated with radiation. Crops and livestock raised in the affected areas tested positive for radiation and had to be destroyed. It was clear the nuclear disaster had terrible effects that would be felt for months and years to come. Today, there is a 12-mile (20-kilometer) zone around the nuclear plant where residents are prohibited from returning though restrictions have been lifted in parts. However, many residents aren't expected to be able to return to their homes for years.

(Below) Members of the American military help clear debris after the tsunami. Countries around the world sent military personnel to Japan's aid.

Environmental Impact

In addition to contamination caused by the nuclear accident, the tsunami also had a huge impact on the environment and wildlife of Japan, as well as areas throughout the Pacific Ocean. Much farmland and many wildlife habitats were severely damaged or destroyed.

Fishing industry

Japan has been regularly testing the amount of radiation in marine animals in the waters off Fukushima since the accident. Because the ocean is a large place, low-level radioactive material is expected to spread out in the water until it is no longer harmful. After the confirmation of a leak of radioactive material into the ocean in August of 2013, fishing was banned off the coast of Fukushima. All other fishing areas in Japan have been declared safe by government agencies, however, the fishing industry in Japan is still struggling against public fear. South Korea, for example, has banned all seafood products from fisheries surrounding the area of the Fukushima plant regardless of whether they meet their own levels of safety or not. To help neighboring countries ease their own fears, the International Atomic Energy Agency is supporting a program in which twenty-four countries in the Asia-Pacific Region are working together to monitor radiation levels in water, plants, and animals and share their results.

More than 110,000 nesting seabirds, including albatross, were killed as a 5-foot (1.5 m) high tsunami wave washed over the Midway Atoll National Wildlife Refuge.

A *giant wave sweeps across Iwanuma, flooding canals and roads and destroying homes and farmland.*

Seawater and silt

Tsunami waves flooded hundreds of square miles of land with seawater. Seawater contains salt. The floodwater also carried **silt** from the ocean. When the water evaporated or drained back to the ocean, it left behind deposits of both salt and silt on land. Salt can enter the groundwater and affect drinking water. Too much salt in soil also makes the land no good for farming.

Japan already suffers from a shortage of land for farming and cannot afford to lose any. Silt buildup also causes problems in canals and on roadways. It needs to be cleared out before transportation routes can operate normally. Flooding can also cause drinking water and sewage systems to overflow into each other causing cross contamination and potential health problems.

23

Worldwide Effects

People around the world felt the effects of the disaster in Japan. The meltdowns at the Fukushima plant raised fears about the safety of nuclear energy and caused other countries to take a closer look at their own plants. It also reinforced how vulnerable communities near the oceans are to natural disasters.

Contaminated water

After the earthquake, Japanese officials, along with those from neighboring countries, worried about the possibility of radioactive water leaking into the ocean. These fears were heightened in August 2013 when officials from the power plant reported that 300 tons of contaminated water had leaked out of a storage tank. Although the water was absorbed by the soil surrounding the plant, there was a strong possibility that it would enter the ground water and eventually reach the ocean. To prevent this from happening, sandbags were placed around the plant. The following October, however, Japanese officials confirmed that 300 tons of contaminated water was actually leaking into the ocean every day. A more permanent solution supported by Japan's nuclear regulator is to surround the plant with an underground ice wall that would prevent contaminated ground water from leaking into the ocean. Another, less popular, option offered was to deliberately leak low-level contaminated water into the ocean at regulated intervals. Small amounts of radioactivity **dissipates** in the vast area of the ocean.

Some of the items that have washed ashore include a small boat in Hawaii, several boat docks in the state of Washington, a restaurant sign in Alaska, and this motorcycle in British Columbia, Canada. The motorcycle's owner in Japan was located and notified.

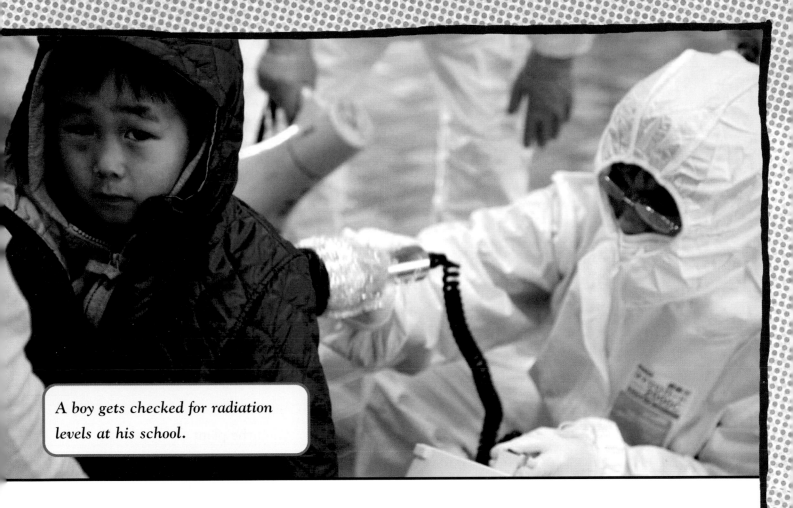

A boy gets checked for radiation levels at his school.

Floating Debris

The Japanese government estimated that 1.58 million tons of debris went into the Pacific Ocean after the tsunami. Some of the debris sank to the ocean floor, but a massive debris field was created. Mostly broken up now, debris has slowly been floating toward North America. Several months after the tsunami, it started washing up on shores up to 3,000 miles (4,828 km) away from Japan. It contains broken wood and building materials, plastics, entire roofs, docks, huge containers, and boats. On the debris, live sea creatures from Japan have been found. These include European blue mussels, Northeastern sea stars, brown algae, fish, and other living organisms. The debris does not contain radiation, but scientists worry that the organisms clinging to the debris might be invasive species that may crowd out native species.

Dangerous Radiation

Following the Chernobyl accident in the former Soviet Union, there was a significant increase in people developing often fatal cancers. While the Fukushima accident was listed at the same severity level as Chernobyl, the high rating was given because there were multiple reactors in jeopardy. The amount of radiation released at Fukushima, however, was not as large as at Chernobyl. In a report in 2013, the World Health Organization reported that the danger of contracting cancer from exposure to the amount of radiation released at the Fukushima plant is very small. The biggest concern is that babies exposed to radiation may develop thyroid cancer in later years. Fortunately, it is one of the most treatable forms of cancer. Doctors do not expect a significant health crisis from the incident.

Other Nuclear Accidents

Before the 2011 Fukushima disaster, the world experienced two other major nuclear accidents: Three Mile Island, in 1979, and Chernobyl, in 1986. To prepare for and prevent potential future emergencies, scientists study past accidents to work toward improving safety features of nuclear power plants.

Three Mile Island

The worst nuclear accident in the United States occurred at one of the two reactors at the Three Mile Island nuclear power plant near Middletown, Pennsylvania, on March 28, 1979. Valves releasing the cooling water were stuck in the closed position resulting in a partial meltdown. Small amounts of radioactive gases were released. No one was killed in the accident and studies suggest long-term health effects have been minimal. The contaminated reactor is permanently shut down, and the fuel has been removed. The plant's other reactor is still being used, and its license to operate expires in 2034

The accident in Pennsylvania led to improvements within the nuclear energy industry that included strengthening of plant designs and equipment, improved emergency procedures and training, and the open sharing of knowledge of nuclear safety with other countries. However, the accident also inspired anti-nuclear energy protests around the world.

In 2012, the United States gave approval for the first new nuclear plant to be built since the Three Mile Island accident.

The contaminated reactor at Chernobyl was encased in concrete. A safer structure is being built to cover it by 2016. The last reactor at the plant was shut down permanently on December 15, 2000.

Chernobyl

The worst nuclear accident to date occurred at the Chernobyl Nuclear Plant in the former Soviet Union on April 26, 1986. A huge buildup of steam and pressure in one of the four reactors led to explosions that blew off the roof of the reactor and set the reactor fuel on fire, sending radioactive material into the air. For ten days, the damaged nuclear plant spewed radioactive materials—the most radiation ever released from a nuclear plant. Trying to keep it secret from the world, the Soviets only admitted to the disaster when neighboring countries detected a huge radioactive cloud drifting over much of Western Europe and the Soviet Union. Two plant workers were killed that day and 28 died a few weeks later from radiation poisoning. About 350,000 people living in the immediate area were evacuated and resettled. Resulting long-term health effects included an increase in cases of thyroid cancer.

It was determined that the disaster at the Chernobyl plant was the result of poor reactor design and serious mistakes made by the plant workers. The accident caused immediate environmental damage. Radioactive waste polluted the water and soil in what are now the countries of Russia, Ukraine, and Belarus. Radioactive particles killed huge numbers of trees in those countries, but the forests are slowly recovering. In Belarus, the government is now allowing resettlement on previously contaminated land. The most important change that resulted from the Chernobyl disaster is the expansion of nuclear safety research to prevent such accidents and to develop ways of managing accidents when they do occur. The International Atomic Energy Agency assists countries, such as Japan, that are affected by nuclear emergencies.

Be Prepared

There is often little or no warning before an earthquake or tsunami. People must immediately find a safe place to be. It is also best to prepare for a long wait for help by stocking a supply of food, blankets, and other materials at home.

Earthquake preparedness

People living in earthquake zones need to have an emergency plan.

1. Find a place in each room of your home where nothing will fall on you.
2. When the shaking starts, drop under a desk or table. Stay away from windows, bookcases, or furniture that can fall.
3. If you're in bed, stay there and cover your head. Don't hang picture frames in places where they can fall on the bed.
4. If you're outdoors, move away from buildings, trees, and power lines, drop to the ground, and cover your head with your arms.
5. Find out where your water valves and gas mains are and know how to turn them off.
6. Emergency kit: keep a supply of canned food, bottled water, battery-operated radios, flashlights, fresh batteries, and first-aid kit.

An earthquake warning is issued when a seismograph registers a P-wave, which is a primary wave that comes roughly 60 to 90 seconds before a stronger, more violent wave.

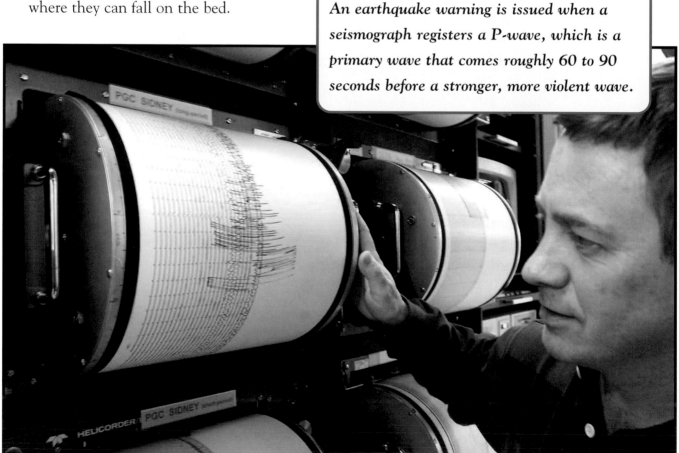

Safety experts recommend stocking a 3-day supply of food, water, and other essential items.

Richter Scale

The Richter scale was invented in 1935. It is a range of the magnitude, or strength, of earthquakes, measured with an instrument called a seismograph. The seismograph has a rotating drum attached to a frame that also holds a pen motionless. During an earthquake, the drum moves with the shaking of the ground, and the pen records that motion on the moving drum. The strongest measurement on the scale is 10.0—a magnitude that no earthquake has ever reached. A 9.0 event, such as the Tohoku earthquake, is considered a "great earthquake," which happens about once every five to 50 years.

Tsunami warning systems

A tsunami warning system detects seismic activity that may trigger a tsunami and issues warnings to the affected areas. It consists of two parts: sensors on buoys in the water or shore-based tide gauges that detect the tsunamis, and a communications system to issue warnings in time for people to evacuate the area. The National Tsunami Warning Center in Palmer, Alaska, covers Alaska, British Columbia, Washington, Oregon, and California. The Pacific Warning Center in Ewa Beach, Hawaii, serves Hawaii and the Pacific-wide area, and is an international warning center for the Pacific Ocean, Indian Ocean, and the Caribbean Sea. When a local center receives a tsunami warning, it broadcasts the warning to the local population so people can evacuate the area.

Nuclear Energy's Fate

After the Fukushima disaster, there was pressure on the Japanese government to change its nuclear policy. A large anti-nuclear demonstration was held in Tokyo six months after the accident. Since then, new legislation has been passed to make power plants safer.

Japan's energy strategy

After the tsunami, people in Japan began calling on the government to phase out nuclear power plants as unsafe. But having to import more oil than usual to make up for the lost supply of nuclear power had cost Japan a great deal of money when the country's reactors were shut down. Before the accident, Japan was on track to increase the percentage of electricity from nuclear energy from 30% to 50% of the country's total.

The government remains torn between the public's lack of confidence in the safety of nuclear energy production and not wanting to become more dependent on energy from oil, which is more costly and creates more pollution. The confirmation in 2013 that contaminated water is leaking into the ocean daily has only increased the pressure to phase out nuclear energy. The government has yet to decide what role nuclear energy will play in Japan's future.

The Onagawa Plant

Of the five nuclear power plants located in the earthquake area, the Onagawa power plant was closest to the epicenter. Although Onagawa experienced similar seismic activity and was hit with the same 42.5-foot (13 m) wave as Fukushima Daiichi, a strong, 46-foot (14-m) high sea wall protected the Onagawa plant from suffering the same fate. The sea wall at the Fukushima Daiichi plant stood only 33 feet (10 m) high. Protection from flooding at Onagawa left six out of eight emergency generators in operation to cool down the plant's reactors. Onagawa's technology and safety features were also twenty years newer than those of Fukushima. Many people hold up the Onagawa plant as an example of how safe the production of nuclear energy has become because it withstood such an extreme event. After the tsunami, the gymnasium at the Onagawa plant was used to shelter more than 300 people left homeless by the wave.

Lessons learned

The accident at Fukushima highlighted several areas that need to be addressed immediately: building higher sea walls to protect plants; finding ways to safely control hydrogen build up; planning for long power outages; and developing new equipment that can withstand earthquakes and tsunamis. The cleanup and revamping of these plants may take as long as 40 years to complete.

The fate of nuclear energy

The accident at Fukushima caused many other countries to reexamine their own nuclear energy policies, as well as the safety of their reactors. Germany has since made plans to close down its entire nuclear energy program by 2022. Belgium, Italy, and Switzerland are also pursuing a nuclear energy phase out. Many Western nations remained unchanged in their nuclear energy policies. Nuclear energy currently accounts for 77% of the United States' total energy and 15% of Canada's total.

Glossary

aftershocks Smaller earthquakes that follow a larger earthquake

cold shutdown The state of a nuclear reactor after cooling below 200 degrees Fahrenheit (95 degrees Celsius)

contamination Something, such as soil, that is made impure or polluted, so is unfit for use

dissipates Spreads out and disappears

foreshocks Mild tremors, or shaking, that occur before an earthquake

magnitude The measurement of the amount of energy released in an earthquake

megathrust An extraordinarily powerful movement in which one tectonic plate is forced under another

meltdown The melting of fuel rods in a nuclear reactor due to overheating

neutron A tiny particle that is smaller than an atom and has no electric charge

radioactive element A pure natural chemical substance that gives off radiation, or energy waves, due to the breaking down of its unstable atoms

rolling blackouts A series of deliberate reductions in power to help ease an overloaded energy production system

seismic waves Energy that travels through the layers of the Earth

silt A mixture of soil and sand

tectonic plates Giant slabs of rock that make up Earth's crust

Index

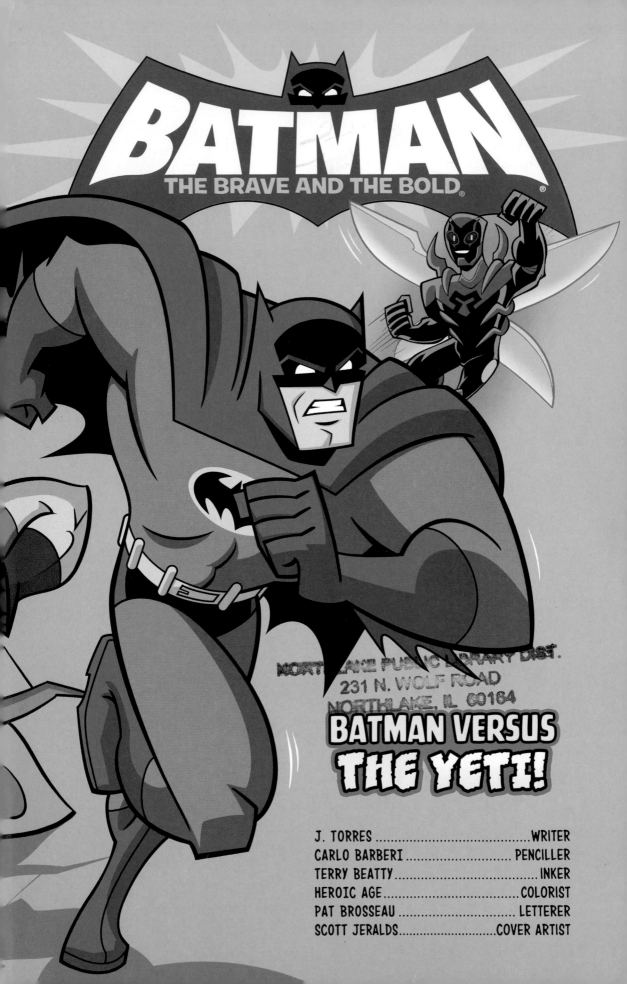

BATMAN
THE BRAVE AND THE BOLD

BATMAN VERSUS
THE YETI!

J. TORRES	WRITER
CARLO BARBERI	PENCILLER
TERRY BEATTY	INKER
HEROIC AGE	COLORIST
PAT BROSSEAU	LETTERER
SCOTT JERALDS	COVER ARTIST

STONE ARCH BOOKS

a capstone imprint

STONE ARCH BOOKS™

Published in 2013
A Capstone Imprint
1710 Roe Crest Drive
North Mankato, MN 56003
www.capstonepub.com

DC Comics
1700 Broadway, New York, NY 10019
A Warner Bros. Entertainment Company

Originally published by DC Comics in the U.S. in single magazine form as Batman: The Brave and the Bold #8.
Copyright © 2013 DC Comics. All Rights Reserved.

Cataloging-in-Publication Data is available at the Library of Congress website:
ISBN: 978-1-4342-4708-7 (library binding)

Summary: Things get hairy when Batman teams up with The Great Ten, China's ultimate super team, in a battle that finds our heroes fighting against an army of yelping Yetis.

STONE ARCH BOOKS

Ashley C. Andersen Zantop *Publisher*
Michael Dahl *Editorial Director*
Donald Lemke & Sean Tulien *Editors*
Heather Kindseth *Creative Director*
Hilary Wacholz *Designer*
Kathy McColley *Production Specialist*

DC COMICS

Rachel Gluckstern & Michael Siglain *Original U.S. Editors*
Harvey Richards *U.S. Assistant Editor*

Printed in China by Nordica.
1012/CA21201277
092012   006935NORD513

CAP 4-243 HP

RRRAAAAAH!

BASH

BASH

BASH

REMARKABLE... FIRST, PHYSICIAN GENERATES *HEAT*, THEN HE MANIPULATES *ICE*...BY MERELY USING HIS VOICE!

I DO NOT SEE ANY REASON TO COMMEND HIS *UNAUTHORIZED* ACTIONS-- ESPECIALLY SINCE WE CANNOT PUT THE AMULET ON HU WEI WHILE HE IS *INSIDE* THAT THING!

WAIT A MINUTE...

...THIS IS *NOT* HU WEI!

WELL, THEN MAYBE...

20

...IT'S HU WEI!

HE'S ALIVE! BUT HE'S COLD AS ICE... PHYSICIAN, CAN YOU HELP HIM?

♪SHHHHHHH♪

MY FATHER WAS A GIFTED SURGEON, BUT EVEN HE WOULD BE AMAZED BY ACCOMPLISHED, PERFECT PHYSICIAN'S SKILLS...

WHERE... WHERE AM I?

WHAT HAPPENED HERE?

AND... IS THAT... BATMAN?

THE GREAT TEN

August General in Iron, Accomplished Perfect Physician, Celestial Archer, and Yeti are only four of China's numerous government-sanctioned Super Functionaries. They use the term "functionary" instead of "hero" to sound more humble. They help protect the Chinese people and their allies in the name of country and duty.

TOP SECRET:
China's answer to the Justice League are its Super Functionaries known as The Great Ten [General, Physician, and Archer are just three of the Ten].

RISING SUN

Izumi Yasunari is the Japanese super hero Rising Sun. His powers include the ability to generate intense light and heat, but he is also an expert in hand-to-hand combat with a black belt in karate. When he's not fighting crime (solo or as a member of the Global Guardians), he works as a solar scientist for Japan's Ministry of Energy and Natural Resources.

TOP SECRET:
Rising Sun always brings wagashi (traditional Japanese sweets) for everyone to snack on at Global Guardian meetings.

CREATORS

J. TORRES WRITER

J. Torres won the Shuster Award for Outstanding Writer for his work on *Batman: Legends of the Dark Knight*, *Love As a Foreign Language*, and *Teen Titans Go*. He is also the writer of the Eisner Award nominated *Alison Dare* and the YALSA listed *Days Like This* and *Lola: A Ghost Story*. Other comic book credits include *Avatar: The Last Airbender*, *Legion of Super-Heroes in the 31st Century*, *Ninja Scroll*, *Wonder Girl*, *Wonder Woman*, and *WALL·E: Recharge*.

CARLO BARBERI PENCILLER

Carlo Barberi is a professional comic book illustrator. He has worked for today's top publishers, such as DC Comics, Marvel, and Dark Horse. His credits include *Batman: The Brave and the Bold*, *Justice League Unlimited*, and *Deadpool*.

TERRY BEATTY INKER

Terry Beatty has been a professional comic book illustrator and inker for many years. His work for DC Comics includes *The Batman Strikes!* and more.

GLOSSARY

amulet [AM·yuh·lit] - any object believed to have power to protect its owner from evil magic or harm

bickering [BIK·ur·ing] - arguing about small or unimportant things

enlighten [en·LITE·uhn] - to teach, reveal, or give understanding to

foreigner [FOR·uhn·ur] - someone from a different country

irreverent [ih·REV·er·uhnt] - disrespectful

restrain [ri·STRAYN] - to hold back or prevent someone from doing something

yeti [YET·ee] - also known as the abominable snowman, a yeti is a monstrous, mythical creature that lives in snowy climate

VISUAL QUESTIONS & PROMPTS

1. In comics books, artists sometimes illustrate characters in solid black ink. Why do you think the artists for this comic book made the character below appear to be in the shadows? What effect does it create? Explain your answer.

2. In comics, artists often use multiple speech balloons connected together instead of one, larger speech balloon. What reasons would the artists have for splitting the speech that this character speaks into three separate balloons?

3. In the panel below, Batman is soaring through the air toward a Yeti. Why do you think the illustrator chose to have the edges of his cape and arm passing over the border of the next panel?

4. On page 12, this panel shows the celestial archer in front of a strange background. Based on the surrounding panels, and what you know about the Celestial Archer, why do you think the artists chose that background for this panel?